COSMIC!

DORSET VOL II

Edited by Carl Golder

First published in Great Britain in 1999 by
POETRY NOW YOUNG WRITERS
1-2 Wainman Road, Woodston,
Peterborough, PE2 7BU
Telephone (01733) 230748

All Rights Reserved

Copyright Contributors 1998

HB ISBN 0 75430 249 0
SB ISBN 0 75430 250 4

FOREWORD

With over 63,000 entries for this year's Cosmic competition, it has proved to be our most demanding editing year to date.

We were, however, helped immensely by the fantastic standard of entries we received, and, on behalf of the Young Writers team, thank you.

Cosmic Dorset Vol II is a tremendous reflection on the writing abilities of 10 & 11 year old children, and the teachers who have encouraged them must take a great deal of credit.

We hope that you enjoy reading *Cosmic Dorset Vol II* and that you are impressed with the variety of poems and style with which they are written, giving an insight into the minds of young children and what they think about the world today.

CONTENTS

Jason Flower	1
Sean Finch	2

All Saints Primary School

Paul Capon	3
Holly Bingham	3
Natasha Chidley	4
Mitchell Cox	4
Amy Northcote	5
James Hayter	5
Abby Carter	6
Philippa Edney	6
Kelly Knott	7
Miles Caswell	7
Peter Martin	8
Caroline Loveless	8
Charlotte Courage	9
Emily Wheeldon	9
Jason Bennett	10
Sam Graham	10
Daniel Adams	11

Christ The King RC VA Primary School

Thomas Maggs	11
Christopher Blackburn	12

Gillingham Milton CE School

George Cadman	13
Ross Alexander	13
Gemma Genge	14
Thomas Knauer	14
Robert Cox	14
Kiarna Tarr	15
Claire Hunt	15
Michael Bendoraitis	16
Lucy Foy	16

Philip Murray	17
Chantelle Johnson	17

Haymoor Middle School
Kristine Tinkler	18

Hill View Primary School
Fiona Monk	18
Sarah Legg	19
Leanne Hill	20
Victoria Vinton	20
Charlotte Dey	21
Natalie Wiseman	22
Perry Wardell-Wicks	22
Leah Trimby	23
Louise Davey	23
Robert Benson	24
Hayley Warren	24
Scott Chislett	25
Adam Young	25
Helen Loveless	26
Ayla Iskender	26
Steven Wade	27
Victoria Brown	27
Matthew Barnes	28
Claire Wilding	28
Kirsty Hunt	29
Gary Antell	29
Joanna Hubbard	30
Phillip Longhurst	31
Fiona Mercer	31
Adam Gritt	32
Rachel Rowland	33
Jack Pilkington	33
Michael Watton	34
Karl Hayman	35
Abigail Parmenter	36
David Jones	36

David Jenkins	37
Craig Livermore	37
Leanne Herridge	38
Luke Sutcliffe	38
Lauren Bliss	39
Louise Scammell	39
Tom Anderson	40
Jake Wentworth	40
Adam Brewer	41
Beth Curtis	42
David Hiscock	42
Nicola Williams	43
Katy Michéle Tanner	44
Luke Baker	44
Ryan May	45

Holy Trinity Junior School

Sara Blackmore	45
Sam Playle	46
Lucy Crabb	47
Sarah Nixon	47
Kristy Wallace	48
Richard Hall	49
Nicholas Goode	50
Simon Holdsworth	50
Alex Harland	50
Fergus Moffatt	51
Terri Sturman	51
Edward Kirk	52
Jake Sorbie	53
Lauren Whitehead	54
Nick Timms	54
Chris Newman	55
Jocelyn Hayne	56
Judy Carruthers	56
James Cooper	57

King's Alfred Middle School
    Martha Henry   58

King's Park Primary School
    Sarah Boussas   58

Milldown Middle School
    Jenny Curl   59
    William Bosworth   60
    Ben Krauss   61
    Juliet Stephenson   61
    Tom Randles   62
    Alex Fowler   62
    Sean Gardiner   63
    Robert Lillington   63
    Peter Bellman   64
    Zoe Whelan   64
    Daniel Palmer   65
    Edward Saunders   65
    Madeleine Barrett   66
    Charlotte Bulpitt   67
    Natalie Seaford-England   67
    Jonathan Edwards   68
    Vicky Crane   68
    Hannah Powell-Bailey   69
    Hayley Moors   69
    Kirsty Upward   70
    Jamie Adams   70
    Sarah Tapper   71
    Hollie Beaumont   71
    Becky Nankervis   72
    Ben Ellis   72
    Charlotte Howell   73
    Charlotte Fowler   74
    Hayley Froud   74
    Kim Cornelius   75
    Katie Royal   76
    Vicki Armstrong   76

David Hamilton-Lawrence	76
Jenny Lawson	77
Joe Chandler	77
Nikki Wade	78
David Judd	78
Emma Christopher	79
Nicholas Stringer	80
Lucy Parsons	81
Matthew Chapman	82
Clive Coats	82
Christopher Kerley	83
Amy Ellis	83
Zara Hanson	84
Tanya Williams	84
Samantha Cooper	85
Hamish Hogg	85
Claire Fowkes	86
Lorelei Dunn	86
Lucy Lake	87
Jade Davis	87
Malcolm Kennedy	88
Katie Booker	88
William Marsh	89
Debi Haines	90
Daniel Sams	90
James Tapper	90
Hephzibah Hickish	91
Sam Galvin	91
Jo Brown	92
Martin Cox	92
Jennifer Hill	93
Samantha Herbert	93
Lisa Scott	94
Mark Murnane	94
Rachel Wells	95
Chris Way	95
Laura Gatehouse	96
Ashley Lock	97

Yan Lyngbo Clerc	97
Nathan Nicholls	98
Richard Ebborn	98
Samantha Francis	99
Darren Rice	99
Vicky Frampton	100
Daniel Harris	100
Gemma Hunt	101
Lemara Bugg	101
Siân Belt	102
Nesta Grant	102
Steven Tankard	102

St Mary's CE VA School, Beaminster
Amy Furness	103
Karen Gibbs	103
Sam Ellis	104
James Ashdown	104

St Osmond's CE School, Dorchester
Gemma Beer	105
Victoria Beer	106

St Thomas Garnet School, Boscombe
Daniel Ingram-Johnson	107
Katherine Saunders	108
Jessica Reeves	108
Amy Stokes	109
Ishaan Chauhan	109
John Henwood	110
Nicholas Baker	110
Alexandra Hixson	111
Lucy Barfoot	112
Charlene Mackin	112
Sarah Linda	113
Thomas Leonard	113
Phillip Sawyer	114
Darren Head	115

Sherborne Preparatory School
    Georgina Timmis   116
    Joshua Edelman   116
    Christopher Ockleton   117
    Ben Bradish-Ellames   117
    Jack Adams   118
    George Smibert   119

THE POEMS

THE IMAGINATION OF THE CLOUDS

I lay on my back on the sand,
And I gazed up towards the sky,
A mosaic of patterns started to form,
As the clouds tumbled and floated by.

The sun was warm on my body,
The sand was gently drying my face,
I felt all alone and relaxed,
As if I had found an empty place.

From behind a cloud a giant came,
And, as strange as this may sound,
No one saw him except me,
His head in the clouds, his feet on the ground.

As the clouds of many colours,
Swirled and swayed and passed by,
The giant roamed across the morning sky,
Then, in a blink of an eye, he was gone.

Day after day I sat on the beach,
Staring at where he had been,
I know no one would believe me,
So I told not a living soul, what I had seen.

Jason Flower (11)

FACTORY CHILDREN POEM

I am a factory child.
I have to get up at 4 o'clock in the morning.
I wish I could get up at 10.

I have to have porridge every morning.
I wish I could have fish.

I have to get the firewood every morning.
I wish somebody else did.

I have only one pair of trousers.
I wish, I wish I had more.

I have to start work at 5 o'clock in the morning.
I wish I could start at nine.

I have to have lunch at 1 o'clock.
I wish I could have it at 12.

I have to put up with the dreadful boss.
I wish he would get the sack.

I have to share my room with three other people.
I wish I had my own room.

I am a factory child,
But I can wish, I can wish!

Sean Finch (11)

FINDING THE COSMIC ZONE

Countdown comes, lift off is bound
Way out in space with no one around.
Time to find the Cosmic Zone
I'll find it before I'm turned to bone.
Cosmic Zone quiet or not?
What's it shaped like, maybe a pot?
Back to earth, nothing's been found
The Cosmic Zone's still up there, undisturbed and sound.

I'm off to find the Cosmic Zone
Off in my rocket named the Cone.
Cosmic Zone different or not?
Is it still shaped like that strange old pot?
Twisting and turning
With my rockets burning.
I'll never find the Cosmic Zone
Before I get there, I'll be turned to bone.

Paul Capon (10)
All Saints Primary School

COSMIC

Here comes cosmic flying through the sky.
The man in a rocket going so high.
Saving planets, going further and further.
Flying past aliens in their flying saucers.
He sees the sun, a hot ball of fire.
He swiftly turns to one side.
And just missing the ball of fire.

Holly Bingham (10)
All Saints Primary School

COSMIC

Looking down at the Earth's beauty
What I can see is . . .
White fluffy clouds, floating slowly across the sky
I look carefully through fluffy shapes
I can see . . .
The greens of holly, apples and grass
The blues of ice, water and rock
Mixed together,
Earth's natural colours
Looking up towards space
What I can see is . . .
The inky blackness of space stretching out for infinity
Flashing, shining, shooting stars,
Sparks of colour shine
The universe, an ordered collection of spinning planets.

Natasha Chidley (10)
All Saints Primary School

COSMIC

Space so calm and silent,
Jupiter's red spot is so bright,
Sun shining on the moon,
Earth is green and blue,
Stars golden-white,
But it's time to go on.

Mitchell Cox (10)
All Saints Primary School

Cosmic

The golden stars sparkle
in the bold black space.
The distant view of planet
earth with the muted colours
of green and blue.

I touch the thin dust on the
misty moon, but I cannot feel
the soft dust because of my
spacesuit.

I leave the quiet and clear
surface to make my long journey
home in my rocket called *Cosmic!*

Amy Northcote (10)
All Saints Primary School

Cosmic

Come and see the moon, a worldly place.
Orange meteorites blasting by in the distance.
Stars painted gold with shiny lining.
Massive craters on the moon.
I've landed on the moon, it is such fun.
Cosmic is great, I love it.

James Hayter (10)
All Saints Primary School

UNTITLED

The floating clouds
in the clear blue sky,
looked cosmically fluffy
with the seagull flying high.

I wish, I wish that I was there,
floating with them
high in the air,
living peacefully without a care.

I could watch the people
in their organised lives,
where everything is just perfect.
I wish, I wish that I was there.

Abby Carter (10)
All Saints Primary School

COSMIC

Looking down at Earth
All the blues and greens
Blend together to make
It look radiant and beautiful.

Soaring high in the sky
Is a meteor with its
Boiling red and orange
Tail flame rushing down
To Earth pulled by gravity
Threatening to explode.

Philippa Edney (11)
All Saints Primary School

COSMIC

The wind rippled the surface of the water and
the fishes darted for cover.
The predator was near, with its sharp pointed fin and
terrifying teeth to attack its prey.

Tiny fish hurtled between the orange and pink
branches, hiding from the threat of destruction.

The coral looked colourful, with twig-like
fronds swaying with the sea.
Tiny microbes supporting underwater life.

A different world down there.
Silent, controlled and undisturbed
yet threatened by man.
But still a world in its own right.

Kelly Knott (11)
All Saints Primary School

THE WORLD

Stars in the sky
they are so high
they're twinkly and bright
in the dark shadowy night
with the planets and moon
and rockets go zoom.

Miles Caswell (10)
All Saints Primary School

COSMIC ZONE

Cosmic Zone is up in space,
That beaming flash in the sky,
I thought what is it like to be there?
I don't know.

I would like to go into space
If I get a chance
Is it lovely, peaceful and calm
Or is it loud and noisy?

I would like to be in space
Just to look around
See what kind of things they have.
Maybe one day.
I will make it up there
I hope so . . .

Peter Martin (10)
All Saints Primary School

COSMIC

People's homes are like a dream.
Everything is always very clean.

Everything is in its pretty place.
So are the stars and planets up in space.

All the objects shining bright.
Some of them reflect the moon's light.

Caroline Loveless (10)
All Saints Primary School

COSMIC

A momentous occasion,
A spectacular sight,
Covered in mist,
With a dim light,
The Earth comes through,
Like a new beginning,
Dawn and then dusk,
The daylight always winning,
Turning gently, hour after hour,
Swirling vapours of green and blue,
Quickly mingling with wispy clouds,
Does it really have nothing to do?

Charlotte Courage (11)
All Saints Primary School

COSMIC

Up in a spaceship,
Looking over to the distance,
I see the horizon and Mars;
Space is full of light shadows,
Dust settles on your boots,
Heavy boots keeping you on the ground,
Strange shapes, mountains, craters, seas,
Ice hiding beneath the surface.

Emily Wheeldon (10)
All Saints Primary School

COSMIC ZONE

The cosmic zone is way up in space,
Over our heads trees and clouds,
I think it is quiet and delightful, peaceful
Or is it loud and noisy like earth?
I'd like to go up there and look around,
For a day or an hour or just for a minute,
To see the planets and the stars in space,
And to see earth in the darkness,
To see the colours blue and green,
And around earth the white fluffy clouds,
And now I've seen the cosmic zone,
I go back to the start, back to earth,
And I shall say again . . .
The cosmic zone is way up in space,
And I'd love to go there.

Jason Bennett (10)
All Saints Primary School

COSMIC

C oming out of earth and into spaceman's spaceship fly.
O n the moon it's full of craters, deep down is water.
S olar system stretches out into infinity shining brightly in the sky.
M an's satellite has travelled space for years looking at planets.
I n the universe stars and planets are far out in space.
C oming back to earth from a long space journey.

Sam Graham (10)
All Saints Primary School

COSMIC

A peaceful place up in space
All the stars are in their place
All the planets spinning round
All the moon rocks on the ground.

The earth green, blue and white
That's all I see from this great height
All the things that are in space
Make it such a terrific place.

Everything is in order
I can see each country's border
Yet war of words are often spoken
Making man's destiny a threatened token.

Daniel Adams (10)
All Saints Primary School

THE LONELY TIGER

A lonely tiger wandering in the forest,
wandering, wandering where would he go?
The tiger came across a lamb,
the lamb had fear in its eyes.
The tiger was getting closer and closer until . . .
the tiger wandered again.

Thomas Maggs (10)
Christ the King RC VA Primary School

Imagine

Imagine if the land was made of paper
Imagine if the sea was made of ink
And the grass was dark blue
And the sky was bright pink!

Imagine if our face was yellow
Imagine if our eyes were square
And our nose was crystal clear
And we had lime green hair!

Imagine if our house was chocolate
Imagine if your cat could bark
And flowers were made of marzipan
And the daytime was dark!

Imagine if money was pebbles
Imagine if animals could talk
And dinosaurs still lived
And we could take them for a walk!

Imagine if there was peace, not war
Imagine if the future we could see
And everyone lived forever more
What a funny world this would be!

Christopher Blackburn (10)
Christ the King RC VA Primary School

WAITING

I just can't wait for my birthday to come.
I just can't wait for Christmas to come.
I can only just wait for my new puppies to come.
I can't wait till I get home tonight.
I can hardly wait until the new year.
My sister can't wait until she gets her Christmas presents
and birthday presents.
Dad can't wait until his next fire call.
Mum can't wait until we have a family party on Christmas day.
I can't wait until I next see my Godmother.
My family can't wait until we get together.

George Cadman (10)
Gillingham Milton CE School

HEDGEHOG

First he finds a home,
Then he finds some food,
His diet is mostly of worms and slugs.
All of this is because of hibernation,
He wanders and roams,
Waddling, scrabbling around.
If he's in danger he becomes a ball,
As spiky as ever,
Ready for spring.

Ross Alexander (10)
Gillingham Milton CE School

THE BROKEN HOUSE

The grass is so long you can't see the windows.
The ivy is creeping slowly up the tattered old walls.
The rusty gate sways and a window creeks as the wind blows softly.
You can hear a faint trickle as the two rivers meet.
The cobbled path becomes loose as the door falls apart.
The broken old house.

Gemma Genge (10)
Gillingham Milton CE School

THE FOX

When I tread through the snow,
it feels like treading through a thick soft white quilt.
When I dig my head in the ground, my whiskers freeze,
I am hoping that I can find something to eat.
With my bushy tail I can find my way home
following footprints behind me.
Colours are drained from the countryside.

Thomas Knauer (10)
Gillingham Milton CE School

FIREWORKS

Whoosh, whiz, bang, sizzle goes a firework.
Up in the sky it whizzes by.
There it goes with a whoosh.
But then explodes in many colours,
red, yellow, orange, blue,
come fluttering down with a great *boom!*

Robert Cox (10)
Gillingham Milton CE School

THE DORMOUSE

The dormouse in his slumber,
On an autumn windy night,
Wrapped up in grass and leaves,
It is a pretty sight.

The shadows of the leaves,
And the cold blowing breeze,
The colours of dawn and dusk,
Floating through the trees.

The dormouse at its rest,
Curls up tightly in his nest,
Eyes closed, paws still,
Knowing that it has had its fill.

Kiarna Tarr (10)
Gillingham Milton CE School

FIREWORKS

Fireworks flickering in the sky,
Bouncing, bouncing, high, high, high,
Crackling colours cascading down,
Different colours red, yellow, brown.

Fireworks whizzing round and round,
Gradually falling to the ground,
Glowing Roman candles burn bright red,
As a firework explodes above my head.

Claire Hunt (11)
Gillingham Milton CE School

The Dormouse In Autumn

The autumn winds come into play,
Chases the little dormouse away.
He piles up dried leaves, dried grass,
And lets the cold autumn pass.
The golden leaves are falling on his nest,
The wet ones are the biggest pest.
Falling conkers can prick him in the side,
But to him in life you cannot hide.
He has no food left in his store,
As more leaves hit the floor.
He's curled up in a little ball,
Ready for the winter snowfall.

Michael Bendoraitis (11)
Gillingham Milton CE School

Autumn Hedgerows

Blackberries in the hedges high.
Wild clematis climbing by.
Ivy in the hedges near.
Green leaves changing colour every year.
Rosy red apples high up in the tree.
Juicy and sweet they look lovely to me.
Conkers all smooth and shiny and brown.
Just waiting to tumble and fall to the ground.

Lucy Foy (10)
Gillingham Milton CE School

FIREWORKS

Boom, bang, whoosh . . . shhh goes the sparkling
red and white fireworks.
The dazzling and screeching sparklers go whizzing by.
The twisting and turning firework goes whizzing, snap,
crackle and pop.
Screaming and beaming go the flashing, whizzing, crackling,
fizzing, yellow and pink fireworks.
The sky high flashing firework goes screaming by.
The light fills up the dark grey, dull sky,
As the glowing rockets whistle by.

Philip Murray (10)
Gillingham Milton CE School

BONFIRE NIGHT

Flashing fireworks going pop,
The bonfire with Guy Fawkes on top,
Different colours red, blue and green,
Cascading down which should be seen.

Flickering lights,
Extremely bright,
Wonderful colours,
What a delight.

Chantelle Johnson (10)
Gillingham Milton CE School

THIS IS MY LIFE!

I try to make this right for you
Just the way that people do,
But when I try to do my best
It always ends up in a mess.
Like when I tried to do long jump,
My friends all got in a hump.
They had a fight for seven days,
It hurt me in so many ways,
Then I said 'Stop your fighting!'
With all my might.
So there you go, that's my story
No one got any glory.

Kristine Tinkler (10)
Haymoor Middle School

VENUS

Venus is purple, yellow and red,
You would not survive there;
You would be dead.

Venus is the second one from the sun,
And can be seen by anyone.

Venus was thought to be earth's twin,
But it's not the right size within:

Venus is also a bright blue,
Pink is its speciality,
No one knew if any planet grew in the beginning.

Fiona Monk (10)
Hill View Primary School

WHEN THE FIRE BELL RANG

We were doing our work
It was silent and still
But I felt a jerk
And almost feel ill

The fire bell rang
Our faces turned white
Our seats from we sprang
And we were out of sight

We ran into line
As fast as we could
No one felt fine
There as we stood

The teacher called out
And she walked through the door
We followed her shout
And then . . . we saw

We saw the red
It was like a coat
It was just a head
There was a lot of smoke

The bright red fire engine came through gates
And parked in the middle of the playground
And then we knew that they weren't late
Silence came and you couldn't hear a sound

The firemen ran
They knew that they could
But I wondered that day
When the fire bell rang.

Sarah Legg (10)
Hill View Primary School

WHEN MY GRAN CAME TO STAY

When my gran came to stay,
we all shouted hip hip hooray.
Last time she came to stay
we took her to the zoo, she wanted
to stay with the kangaroos, but when
we came back, she had eaten the whole zoo.

The year before we took her to
Polton's Park and she wanted to
have an ice-cream.
We were first in the queue, gran demanded
that she had the whole box of chocolate ice-cream,
but the ice-cream man yelled back,
'I'm sorry that's not allowed'
but my gran didn't care so she kicked him in the air.

This year we hoped to do something nice,
and we did, we took her to a nature park.
For the first half an hour she was as quiet as can be
then she wandered off and she ate a lot of bugs.
When we got home she was as sick as can be.

Leanne Hill (10)
Hill View Primary School

FRIENDS FOREVER

All our secrets shared
For each other we've cared
If our dreams shall come true
I shall owe it all to you

Our arguments and tears
But all through these years
We've stayed together
Our friendship will last forever.

Victoria Vinton (10)
Hill View Primary School

THE LITTLE BEE

One day on a summer's morning,
The bees were buzzing around.
The bees from the trees stood on their knees
And fell to the ground.

The bees stood up
And flew away, ready for another day.
A bee was left all small and shaken.
He really had had a big fall.

He stood up and wobbled around,
The other bees were nowhere to be found.
He searched and searched
But found no trace,
Then he saw a resting place.

Inside a tree all soft and warm,
Just the place for a weary bee,
He found some moss and snuggled down.
'I will look for the bees another time'.
Then all at once with a blink of an eye, the bee was sound asleep.

Charlotte Dey (11)
Hill View Primary School

GIRLS

Some girls have curls,
In their golden hair,
Some girls do twirls
Dancing in the air.

> Some girls play football,
> And all other sports,
> Some girls play rugby
> In their funky shorts.

Some girls wear mini skirts,
And really high shoes,
Some girls are show offs
And should be put in a zoo.

> But me, I'm totally different,
> Because I'm not even a girl.

Natalie Wiseman (11)
Hill View Primary School

THE MENACINGLY EAGLE

Flying, flying, flying high.
Into the deep blue sky it gleams.
Swirling, twirling, shimmering and glimmering.
The prey awaits.
The eagle looking deadly and vicious.
Waiting for the kill.
Its eyes blazing in the sun.
Then suddenly the eagle dives menacingly, powerfully.
Then the eagle hits the prey, fiercely and the prey is killed.

Perry Wardell-Wicks (11)
Hill View Primary School

BROTHERS

I walk in the front door,
And there he is,
Waiting for me in the hall.
My brother wants me to play football.

I make him get down on his knees
And beg, then I give in.
I go outside when I've got changed
But I know, and he knows that I'm gonna win.

It's been five minutes now,
And he's winning four-three,
But I don't really care
'Cause I'm being really kind,
And letting them in.

Leah Trimby (10)
Hill View Primary School

OUR UNIVERSE

It started with an explosion,
Bang! Smash! Bang! Crash!
After that very moment the universe was made,
Stars, sun, planets and more.
Venus, they call the morning star,
Mars, the red planet with no life at all,
Uranus and Saturn with rings galore.
This is just a spot of our Universe,
There is a lot more.

Louise Davey (10)
Hill View Primary School

THE NIGHT

The moon shining brightly,
His face looking down on me,
Glistening stars scattered across the sky,
Like diamonds bright,
Animals crying crisp and clear,
Roaring sea screaming loud and clear,
Rolling hills shining silver in the moonlight,
Trees whispering to each other,
Standing tall and grey,
Their branches crooked and twisted,
A gleaming blue stream,
Trickling down the hillside,
Meandering to the sea,
The night seems to me,
To be the beautiful place there could be.

Robert Benson (11)
Hill View Primary School

GREEN

Green on the grass.
  Green in the sea.
    Green on the leaves in the trees.
      Greens on jumpers.
        Greens on shoes.
          Green on background.
          Green's on blues.

Hayley Warren (10)
Hill View Primary School

Rugby

Rugby is a good sport
It takes a lot of skill
Running down the touch line
You're sure to get a thrill.

Your first aim is to get a try
Then for a conversion
You have to kick high.

But if you've lost
Or if you've won
It doesn't matter
It's still a lot of fun.

Scott Chislett (11)
Hill View Primary School

The Night

The moon glares at you, its colour is white
The stars shine bright for it is the night
The wolves howl
The screeching is an owl.

People sleep and count sheep
In the darkness is where the planets are left to sleep
And in the blackness all you see is night.

Adam Young (10)
Hill View Primary School

WHEN THE MICE COME OUT

Nobody's about,
When the mice come out,
Everyone's sleeping,
Nearby the cats are creeping.

The night is dark all around,
Mice all on the ground,
Each one with a scared look on their face,
Unhappy to be in this race.

Each one decides where to go,
High or low nobody knows,
Some go this way, some go that,
Don't want to be caught by the vicious cats!

Helen Loveless (10)
Hill View Primary School

FLOWERS

Waving in the soft light breeze,
Tulips are colourful as can be,
The petals are so soft,
The stem is a wonderful green,
There's a hint of gold in the middle.
The sun is bright,
But what I love,
Most of all,
Is the
Smell.

Ayla Iskender (10)
Hill View Primary School

KEEP THE COUNTRYSIDE CLEAN

C lean is cool,
L et's be cool,
E at our food,
A nd put the wrappers away.
N ewts and fish want to live too.

O n school trips pick up litter,
U nder the ground,
R abbits and rodents want to live too.

C ool is the word,
O f the countryside,
U p in the sky, birds like to fly,
N imble and quick,
T hey like it up there,
R ooks and ravens want to live too,
Y es, keep the countryside clean!

Steven Wade (10)
Hill View Primary School

LOVELY HORSES

White horses galloping through the muddy fields,
Horses, lovely horses,
Big metal hooves thumping on the soggy ground,
Saddles are flying up and down,
As they gallop through the muddy field.

Victoria Brown (10)
Hill View Primary School

GREEN

Green is a bright and dark colour.
It shows up in the dark with a torch.
It is the colour of a sweet.
Some people wear green because they like it.
Everyone wears green when they go to school.
Green is quite popular with everyone.
Leaves are green.
My bunk beds are green.
A cat outside looks dark green, but it is black.
The house looks dark green.
At night I am frightened by the dark.
In the morning it was green.
I first thought it was a green dream!

Matthew Barnes (11)
Hill View Primary School

SUN, SEA, SAND AND THE SEASHORE

The sun shines down on us,
The sea rushes to the shore,
The sand is soft and comforting,
And the seashells crackle more.

The sun shines on our faces,
Giving us a healthy glow,
The sun's glistening and inviting,
Everything's so happy and no one wants to go.

Claire Wilding (10)
Hill View Primary School

PEOPLE

People are tall
People are strong
People are weak
And people are small.

People are thick
People are brainy
People are clean
And people are smelly.

People are ugly
People are happy
People are moody
And people are thin

And people are almost everything.

Kirsty Hunt (10)
Hill View Primary School

THE CRAB

A crab
lurking in the depths of the sea
waiting, waiting to pounce on its prey
waiting, waiting and suddenly
it pounces on an exploring fish
slowly, slowly the crab digests the fish
after that he goes in his hide and comes back out
but an octopus is waiting, gulp, bye-bye crab.

Gary Antell (11)
Hill View Primary School

GOODBYE DADDY

Goodbye Daddy,
Love you,
Hope to see you soon,
See you on a Sunday,
And maybe on a
Wednesday,
Love you.

Goodbye Daddy,
I wish you wouldn't go,
I'm really going to miss you,
See you on a Sunday
And maybe on a
Wednesday,
Love you.

Goodbye Daddy,
I bet you will come back,
But then you might not,
See you on a Sunday,
And maybe on a
Wednesday,
Love you.

Joanna Hubbard (11)
Hill View Primary School

SCARDY CAT

Children of the night be careful
There's something stalking you.

Children of the night,
Don't you look back, green eyes watch.

Children of the night,
Hurry start running to your home.

Children of the night,
Look back and smile as Tiger
Your cat looks up at you.

Phillip Longhurst (11)
Hill View Primary School

IN THE LOFT

There I am all alone
Up in the loft
Spiders crawling
Up my leg
I'm shivering.

I hear someone coming
Up the steep stairs
Go away!
Someone opens the creepy door
It is only my mum.

Fiona Mercer (10)
Hill View Primary School

WHY DO WE HAVE TO DO HOMEWORK?

Why do we have to do homework?
We do enough at school!
Why do we have to do homework?
I think it's a bit cruel!

                    Why do we have to do homework?
                    I'd rather play a game
                    Why do we have to do homework?
                    It really is a pain.

Why do we have to do homework?
We should just go out and play
Why do we have to do homework?
Why can't we play all day?

                    Why do we have to do homework?
                    Especially if we're at home
                    Why do we have to do homework?
                    We do it all on our own.

Why do we have to do homework?
It takes up half an hour!
Why do we have to do homework?
We should do it in our school hours.

                    Why do we have to do homework?
                    Especially if it's boring
                    Why do we have to do homework?
                    Why can't we just do drawing?

Why do we have to do homework?
I'd rather watch TV
Why do we have to do homework?
It doesn't seem right to me.

Adam Gritt (10)
Hill View Primary School

SPACE DREAM

Far away in a dream one night
I sat in a rocket and took flight.

I flew into space and saw the stars
Visited Mercury, Venus and Mars.

I landed on Saturn and went skating on its rings,
Saw countless aliens and extra terrestrial things.

I stopped off in Jupiter and played a game of football,
With some friendly aliens who reached 14 feet tall.

I hitched a quick ride home on a shooting star
And thought about my adventures and how I'd travelled far.

I realised in the morning, I'd actually flown to space
For I'd won a trophy in the star-to-star rocket race.

Rachel Rowland (11)
Hill View Primary School

I PLAY FOOTBALL

I play football every day
It gives me joy and makes me gay
I have a shot, I hope to score
Then I hear a great big roar
Fans and players chant my name
Because I have just won the game.
Everyone's trying to sign me up
I know I'll be rich soon enough
It's got to be Man U in the end
You can't keep me off the pitch.

Jack Pilkington (10)
Hill View Primary School

SEASONS

Look out of the window,
Imagine what it will be like in spring,
The flowers coming into blossom,
And hear the birds sing,
Watch the dainty petals,
Sparkle with the dew,
See the sun bright and early,
And the sky covered with blue.

Look out of the window,
Imagine what it will be like in summer,
Feel the soft gentle breeze,
Sounds like it's calling to its mumma,
See the grass as an emerald,
People sunbathing on the beach,
Sand as rich as the inside of a peach.

Look out of the window,
Imagine what it will be like in autumn,
Watch the leaves fall off the trees,
The wind has obviously slaughtered 'em
Under the trees a mat of crispy leaves,
But look on the other side,
There's evergreens full of colour,
With the red, orange and pink sky.

Look out of the window
Imagine what it will be like in winter
With all the white snow
You could be touching a tree with splinters
Wrap up tight
Without a fight
Because the North Wind can blow.

Michael Watton (10)
Hill View Primary School

JULES RIMET

July 12 1998,
At the Stad de France, spectators await.
They've won the Jules Rimet five times together,
Scorching in skill, scorching in weather.

England v Brazil,
The best v *the* best.
England are better than the others,
And Brazil are better than the rest.

The match has started,
Hip-hip-hooray!
This is bound to be,
Match of the day!

Roberto Carlos' free kick,
Nearly breaks the net.
Brazil have scored,
Please England, don't fret!

McManaman beats five,
He's never tense,
He scores the equaliser
That makes sense.

A Brazilian defender,
Shows Gascoigne his fist.
Owen converts
He's on the scoring list!

England win,
Result's 2-1
England have won the World Cup.
That was fun!

Karl Hayman (10)
Hill View Primary School

NIGHT LIGHTS

'Good night,' said Mum.
'Turn off the light!'
Once the lights are out
My imagination mucks me about.

I carefully climb out of my bed
If I am able
To move swiftly across the room
Without knocking the table
I open the curtains and I stare into the night
I look at the emptiness
And see that the moon is shining bright
I think to myself
Another night light.

Abigail Parmenter (10)
Hill View Primary School

THE UNEXPECTED WEATHER

The drifting snow,
Coming on hard,
Blocking car entrances.

      Raining cats and dogs,
      Like buckets of rain,
      Pouring out all at once.

           Finally the snow melts,
           The rain disappears,
           Then the sun shines.

David Jones (11)
Hill View Primary School

FIRE, FIRE

Fire, fire
Burning bright
Fire, fire
In the night
Why have
You just set
My house
Alight?

Burning flame
I just saw
Some smoke
Up from the
Floor
Suddenly
The door
Slammed and
There was no
More.

David Jenkins (10)
Hill View Primary School

SPACE

S tars that shine in the sky,
P lanets with moons.
A steroids heading for the sun.
C omets with lit up tails.
E arth the planet with life.

Craig Livermore (10)
Hill View Primary School

SUPERMUM

Supermum cooks, she cleans too,
Supermum does everything for you,
Supermum drives us around everywhere
Just so you can meet your friends down Bournemouth Square.
She brings you food in front of TV
So you can watch TOTP
She lets you stay up till one in the morning,
Because she's in a deep sleep, snoring.
Supermum is cool,
She's not too tall,
She's just about right
She gives us chips every night
But let's just say I love *my mum*
She's the best in every way
Much more than words could ever say.

Leanne Herridge (11)
Hill View Primary School

THE ALIENS ARE HERE

The aliens are here,
And there gummy,
The kids want their mummy.

The aliens are here
They made a face
And frightened the place.

The aliens had a quiver
We had a shiver 'cause
We both showed a photo
And all ran to Pluto.

Luke Sutcliffe (10)
Hill View Primary School

THE QUEEN OF HEARTS

The 31st of August was such a tragic day,
We woke to the news that
Princess Diana had died that day
The people came and the flowers too
Outside the palace the carpet grew.

Surely, we thought, it couldn't be true,
But when we saw the car we really knew
That our pretty princess had been taken away
To live with the angels far away.

She cared for the sick, the young and the old
And now she has gone we must be bold
We'll look after the boys, both Harry and Wills
In them she will live until they grow old.

She's the queen of our hearts
And will always be here
We still love her dearly
Of that we are clear.

Lauren Bliss (11)
Hill View Primary School

MARS

Space is full of planets and stars
There is a planet called Mars
On the planet Mars
(They do not drive cars.)
Aliens look like chewy bars
When they're from the planet Mars.

Louise Scammell (10)
Hill View Primary School

POLLUTION

Crisp packets, wrappers, cans and sweets,
Are usually the things that you find on the streets.
People throw them away without a care,
Usually throwing them anywhere.

There's a great invention called a bin,
It's meant to be used for throwing rubbish in.
Nobody notices that it's there,
So they find a nice spot and drop their litter there.

Soon the world will be gone,
Thanks to all of the pollution.
But if you would like to prevent this happening,
You should try using something like a bin.

Tom Anderson (11)
Hill View Primary School

MY NAN IS 93

My Nan is 93
She is still as active as she used to be
She takes me to the fairground
We sometimes have a laugh
Then she takes me home again
And gives me quite a bath.

My Nan is 93
She's not as active as she used to be
She takes me to get her pension
Although I've got to mention
She gives me half her pension.

Jake Wentworth (10)
Hill View Primary School

LIVERPOOL WERE...

Liverpool were two-nil up
When Fowler struck
The crowd went wild
The crowd went mad
And all the opposition looked sad.
There's five minutes to go
When they were clear and the Goalie was close to tears.
They worked hard to get back and then, *smack*!
The ball went flying and it hit the bar
The Goalie relieved, the Manager was pleased
And all the crowd roared at what Liverpool had done.

'We have got to win today.'
That was hard for the manager to say.
United had the first chance
The Goalie was in a trance.
The ball hit the post
And bounced out again.
There was a minute to go
Fowler took a shot
The Goalie went low
But not low enough.
The ball went in with a thud
And all that was left was a stud.

Adam Brewer (10)
Hill View Primary School

IF I LIVED ON . . .

If I lived on Mars,
I would stare at the stars,
I'd build a rocket, drive out into space,
And travel to each planet, place to place.

If I lived on Pluto,
I might like it a lot though,
Maybe I'd just want to get away,
I can't really say.

If I lived on Saturn,
I'd run around the ring,
Or maybe I'd just skate,
And never ever be late.

But I live on Earth,
And glad of it I am too,
Because I like it here,
And I know what to do.

Beth Curtis (10)
Hill View Primary School

LITTER

There must be some kids I guess,
Who like to see my school a mess,
This behaviour makes me mad,
The culprits must be really sad.

The kind of kids who throw down litter,
Make me really, really bitter,
What kind of state would we be in,
If no one used a litter bin.

David Hiscock (11)
Hill View Primary School

TEACHERS

Some teachers are funny,
Some teachers are sad,
Some teachers crack jokes,
Which are very, very bad.

Some teachers are strict,
Some teachers are nice,
Some teachers have hair,
That look like rice.

They come to teach you,
To work you like mad,
They think you are silly,
You're not too bad.

When you go home,
At the end of the day,
You think you've suffered,
Teachers shout, 'Hooray!'

Nicola Williams (10)
Hill View Primary School

WHEN I GROW UP

When I grow up I think I'll be,
A policeman on duty.
Or I could be a shopkeeper,
And sell oranges, *cor, they're so juicy!*

I could be a bank manager,
And handle lots of money,
Or I could be a comedian,
And be very funny!

Or shall I have a sports car,
And live in a mansion,
I could go and find myself a prince,
Who is very handsome!

Or I could win the lottery,
And be very rich,
Or I could be an explorer,
And fall in a ditch!

For the more a girl lives,
The more a girl learns,
I think I'll be all of them,
By taking them in turns!

Katy Michéle Tanner (10)
Hill View Primary School

MARS

M any planets in our Solar System,
A pproaching Earth like a bullet,
R ockets zooming past,
S hooting stars zooming past.

Luke Baker (10)
Hill View Primary School

WATER!

Water, water gentle water,
Swiftly crashing waves.
Crashing waves hit the ground
Like a flash of lightning striking down.
Water is gentle
Water is clear
Water is a magic trick trying to reappear.

Ryan May (10)
Hill View Primary School

SPACE

The space up there is
    The colour black,
It's like being stuck
    Inside a sack.

With cratered planets
    And twinkling stars,
There are no human beings
    Or any fast cars.

A ball of gas which
    Is called the sun,
Which to me looks
    like a sticky bun

With planets going
    Round at a steady pace,
There's nothing like our
    Deep dark space.

Sara Blackmore (11)
Holy Trinity Junior School

EVIL ALIEN'S SCREAMS

Chilling winds soar about
High-pitched screams and whistles
Instant flashes from the moon
Caused by explosions from missiles.
Larger rays come down
Starships zoom through the sky
Aliens come to land
But their craft are hovering high.

Slowly they knock down the door
Creeping up the long stairs
Slime drooling off their skin
Sticking down all the hairs.
Then they open your door
Slithering into your room
Moving over the floor
Surely sealing your doom.

As they jump on your bed,
Their mouths begin to drool,
Then they force open the window
With a special kind of tool.
Then they all become a blur,
At last, they're not going to rule!
When suddenly you wake up,
'You'll soon be late for school!'

Sam Playle (10)
Holy Trinity Junior School

ALIEN ATTACK

It's time for the alien attack,
Little green men with hundreds of eyes,
All of them are here women and guys,
So flee your country flee your lands,
But can you escape their icy hands?
Up from the stars they come in their ships,
From a lonely dark planet called Blips.
They go past Saturn and its great rings,
Thinking, 'Must be careful of those things!'
As they drew closer to our big Earth,
They rolled around on the floor in mirth,
As they saw the size of our planet,
They said, 'Oh no it can't be. Can it?
It didn't seem like this in the book,
Come on let us have another look
For the one we want to get
Because this isn't the best one yet!'
So the green aliens retreated,
Feeling that they had not completed,
Their search for best holiday planet.
For their race of the great green gannet!

Lucy Crabb (10)
Holy Trinity Junior School

THE RED ROCKET

I went to space in my red rocket,
I saw these two yellow lights.
I went a bit closer to the yellow lights.
It was an alien in a car
An alien in a car, I started to laugh.
Ha, ha, ha!

Sarah Nixon (10)
Holy Trinity Junior School

THE ALIEN'S TRIP TO EARTH

Every time a little green man,
Goes past the window in a frying pan,
It goes whizzing through the sky,
It flies very, very high,
Until it will land on some cheese.

Flashing lights at very great heights,
Come flying in to land.
Buzzing noises, and opening of doors,
The spaceship gives a great loud roar.

Aliens file out,
And start walking about,
To see what they can find,
Green antennae, and long red capes,
Beep, beep, beep, means, 'Oi, look mate.'

Test tubes full - job is done,
Tubes are loaded, by the tonne.
Back up to space, the ship will go,
Circling the stars, with what they know.

The alien's trip, was a total success,
Now they know, a lot which they can express,
'Goodbye for now,' the aliens say,
'See you next year, maybe in May.'

Kristy Wallace (10)
Holy Trinity Junior School

NON-GRAVITY FOOTBALL

The whistle blew,
The ball went through
Non-existent space.

It came to a Star City's defender
And he kicked it up field in wonderful splendour
The forward latched on to it
But bit by bit it went out for a goal kick.

The pure white ball was hoofed up field,
A bit too far on to one of Starship Enterprise's shields,
The ball bounced back with a loud whack,
Into the ref's arms for the end of the first half.

In the second half Space Shuttle United kicked off
The player played it back
But the player was hacked
He took the free kick
With a mighty high flick
The forward was chasing after the ball
The keeper in front of him was big and tall.

The player did a cheeky skill round the keeper
And tapped it in the goal
The ref blew his whistle for full time
And Space Shuttle United has done quite fine.

Richard Hall (11)
Holy Trinity Junior School

OUT IN SPACE

Out there is a dark and gloomy, wonderful place called space.
Floating stars and a planet called Mars,
There are spaceships with bright, bright lights every night
And green, mean aliens.
It's a great place,
It's a wonderful dark and gloomy place
Out in space.

Nichola Goode (10)
Holy Trinity Junior School

COSMOS

Shooting through the starry sky,
Into darkness beyond the clouds.
Stars shine like little diamonds,
I'm soaring into space unknown,
Everything is still and quiet,
Heaven is beautiful.

Simon Holdsworth (10)
Holy Trinity Junior School

COUNTING STARS IN SPACE

Sitting in your garden
With a cup of tea,
Counting all the stars
That you can see.
'Don't miss that one.'
'Look at this one.'
But they're all the same
And there's no one to blame.

Alex Harland (11)
Holy Trinity Junior School

SURVIVAL

Water on the moon the scientists say,
How do they know anyway?

Could us humans live on the moon,
Or would we die much too soon.

Could we live upon Mars,
Maybe we'd meet aliens in bright yellow cars.

Could we live on the planet Saturn,
The one with a ring for its pattern.

I can name one planet we can live on right now,
But the question is, who invented these planets and how.

Fergus Moffatt (10)
Holy Trinity Junior School

STARLIGHT

Starlight, Moonlight,
Isn't it bright tonight?

Star-glow, Moon-glow,
Doesn't the night go slow?

Star-shine, Moon-shine,
Jupiter of moons has nine.

Star-blend, Moon-blend,
It's time for night to end.

Terri Sturman (10)
Holy Trinity Junior School

LIFT-OFF

The kids gave a cheer,
When he climbed in his gear,
Then he climbed in his craft,
With his wife, the other half.
He put on his belt,
And he gave a yelp,
When his other half,
Climbed out of the craft,
Having kissed her goodbye,
He gave a cry,
Because he didn't want to go,
As he loved her so.
5, 4, 3, 2, 1, lift off,
Zooooom!
And he's off to see the moon,
His heart gave a lurch,
When he left the Earth,
He soon,
Saw the moon.
Having landed the craft,
He got on with the task,
Of doing the job,
He had on his log.
After his tea,
He went for a pee,
With a blast of his rockets,
His eyes popped out of their sockets,
And he found himself,
Back at home.

Edward Kirk (11)
Holy Trinity Junior School

MY DREAM IN SPACE

I lie in my bed awake at night,
With the curtains open, so there's a glow of light.
Dreaming that I could be flying in space,
Whooshing around with no sign or trace.

In my dream I am whooshing, flying so free,
Floating around, with wilderness and glee.
I look up, and suddenly, I begin to dip,
Then I realise, I'm in a spaceship.

I'm flying so high, passing bright stars,
Dodging small planets, ready for a quick stop on Mars.
I jump out of the spaceship, then I stub my toe,
So I jump back in the spaceship, and like a bullet off we go.

I dodge past stars, heading for the Moon,
Then it begins to get hot, as if it was June.
I was burning up now, like a hot cross bun,
Then I soon realised, I was heading for the sun.

In a panic, I turned the spaceship around,
By this time the bugs on the floor, were in a sweat puddle and drowned.
I was hoping that I'd get there real soon,
In the distance I could see the glowing bright Moon.

It started to wobble, then it was heading straight down,
I was going to crash, into the ground.
We were now going faster, were going to land in the streams,
Then I woke up and realised, it was all just a dream.

Jake Sorbie (10)
Holy Trinity Junior School

SPACE!

When rockets go to the moon,
They take off with a boom!
They see planets such as Mars
And millions and millions of stars
Saturn with its rings so bright
The sun that gives us our daily light.

The astronauts exploring space
Are amazed at this wonderful place
Pluto is so very cold
But on some planets you have to hold your nose!

Lauren Whitehead (11)
Holy Trinity Junior School

SPACE

Space is a place,
Maybe it's got a different race,
A race of green men,
Having a chase,
On another planet or place,
Maybe men with an orange face,
And a blue body, what a case,
But we don't know what happens in space.
Space is a place.

Nick Timms (1)
Holy Trinity Junior School

INTERGALACTIC FOOTBALL

Playing football in space,
With my friend Dennis McNace,
'What a strange place,'
Said Dennis, nicknamed McNace.

Dennis had a lot of wit,
Playing football in space.
He made a bad tackle, now I'm sort of unfit,
He should be sent off this place.

As I made a turn,
I call it 'the Chris Waddle',
From that Dennis will learn,
I should be picked by Glen Hoddle.

I took a kick, I made it bend,
Then Dennis caught it and threw,
I thought that was something he couldn't defend,
Then his whistle blew.

I pressed the button in the socket,
Then we travelled home,
Then we sped up in our brilliant rocket,
To go to our key-camp in Rome.

Chris Newman (10)
Holy Trinity Junior School

COSMIC

5, 4, 3, 2, 1, Lift Off . . .
Apollo 13 has hit the sky ever so high
Gravity holding it hurtling back into planet air
Apollo 13 and its crew have landed on the moon too soon,
Not like the real life story.
Little green aliens in their little fitted suits who live on the moon.
The little green aliens so fat and squishy invited
The crew to sleep and eat (so they can eat them)
In the morning there was just flesh and bones
Where the crew had eaten every one.

Jocelyn Hayne (10)
Holy Trinity Junior School

OUT OF THIS WORLD

Above the sky above the sea,
There's no place I would rather be,
There's planets and stars for you to see,
There is no door, there is no key,
Come and go, you are free.

Don't try to eat or drink a drink,
It will only float away,
Instead just look at the Martians play,
They're out and about all day.

Judy Carruthers (11)
Holy Trinity Junior School

SPACE RACE

Bang! Went the rocket launchers
Bang! Bang! Boom!
Fizz! Went the second rocket
Off we zoom!

Now we're all in mid-space
Waiting for the rocket race
We're still here waiting, waiting to go
We're waiting for the chequered flag, that's when we will know.

And off we go I'm in the lead
Behind me a massive great stampede
One crashes into Venus, another into Mars
But I'm still in the lead, zooming past shining stars.

Someone's coming up, they're nearly neck and neck
So I say, 'Missile.' Computer says, 'Check.'
Fizz! Goes the missile off it really zooms.
Then it hits the other spaceship and makes a massive boom!

Then I see an important sign
Otherwise called the chequered line
And I know I've nearly won
But I pressed the wrong button and I'm heading to the sun.

Sizzle! Goes the rocket launcher
Sizzle! Sizzle! Boom!
Sizzle goes the second rocket
Then we go *boom, oops.*

James Cooper (10)
Holy Trinity Junior School

AUTUMN

Autumn, autumn here it comes
So say goodbye to the big hot sun
Red, yellow, bronze and brown
All these colours floating around
As leaves twirling, twisting down,
Till they reach the leaf-covered ground
Birds migrate
Animals hibernate
This is autumn.

Frost and ice
Still autumn's nice
Chestnuts cracking
People backing
Away from cold winds blowing
Who knows when it might start snowing?
People put on extra socks
Autumn's full of surprises and shocks
This is autumn.

Martha Henry (10)
King Alfred's Middle School

HAPPINESS POEM

Happiness is bright yellow like the warm sun.
Happiness tastes like sweet ice-cream and lots of fun.
Happiness smells like flowers on their bed and the smell of cherries
freshly picked.
Happiness looks like a sparkly stream. Twinkles and makes us dream.
Happiness sounds like birds in the sky and when they fly.
Happiness feels like soft skin and wins all the time.
Happiness is a good rhyme.

Sarah Boussas (10)
King's Park Primary School

A WORLD FOR THE FUTURE

What'll the future bring,
Will we still dance and sing,
Will we be robot like,
Will we all ride a trike?
Or will we zoom through space,
In a suitcase,
Or will we zoom through the air,
On a flying pear?

We might you know,
We could you know.
It's true.

But if you listen you can hear the earth, say 'Help me now,
Blowing up the planet isn't something that deserves a bow,
Think of all the animals, think of the trees,
Think of the daffodils, and the gentle breeze.
Stop and think what you're doing, *please.*
Stop, and think what you're doing, *please.*'

In other words, stop, put your weapons down,
Doesn't matter if you're white, black or brown,
And if you want earth to be here in a thousand years,
So you can still enjoy a couple of beers,
Join hands, be friends,
And help each other overcome the bends.

We can you know,
We can you know,
It's true.

Jenny Curl (10)
Milldown Middle School

A WORLD FOR THE FUTURE

If you're worrying about the earth,
While you're sitting by the hearth,
You have due course to be worried,
But the world's not being hurried.
We're affected by pollution,
But also by evolution.

It will get us out of this rut,
But there are a lot of 'buts',
There are many in this poem,
So I'd better get going,
And tell you about our planet,
And how we're going to harm it.

Dumping oil in the ocean,
Getting millions of cars in motion,
Putting fire in the forests,
Do any of these and we're for it,
So make your tankers unsinkable,
Or the result will be unthinkable.

Instead of a car, use a bus,
And it will save a lot of us,
And don't fire up the woods,
Even though I know you could,
It would do a lot of damage,
Lots of habitats would be savaged.

The moral of this story is:

Beware and take care!
Your stupidity could mean our destruction!

William Bosworth (10)
Milldown Middle School

A WORLD FOR THE FUTURE

The world for the future should be rid of hunger,
No starving people any longer.
Plenty of rain to make the plants grow,
Fields of crops, row upon row.

The world for the future should be rid of pollution,
Scientists trying to find a solution.
Cars for the future will be powered by sun,
Clean air to breathe for everyone.

The world for the future should be rid of war,
No fighting or arguing anymore.
Harmony worldwide all living together,
Lasting peace forever and ever.

Ben Krauss (11)
Milldown Middle School

BOYS

Boys, they only have one toy
A football, that's a boy
Off the football pitch they come
With a very muddy bum.

They find a keeper
Lose a weeper
Then they win the game.

Red in cheers
Won the game
The rest in tears
Leeds lost the fame.

Juliet Stephenson (10)
Milldown Middle School

A WORLD FOR THE FUTURE

If we used solar power, and put it on a very high tower,
The panels would catch the sun and give us energy,
Hour after hour.

If we could catch the water flow,
We could make hydro-electric power,
Go and go.

If we used the power of wind,
To turn the turbine on the hill,
Day after day.

If we used clean electric power,
To power our transport and our homes,
There would be fresh, clean air, year after year.

If we blew up all the big power stations,
That give out gas, coal and nuclear fumes,
And then, it might be, that our planet is pollution free.

Tom Randles (10)
Milldown Middle School

A WORLD FOR THE FUTURE

In the future there will be computers everywhere
All your answers will be under a button
In the summer holidays we will be going to the moon
Every car will be environmentally friendly
All transport will be solar powered
So think of the world and its future.

Alex Fowler (11)
Milldown Middle School

A WORLD FOR THE FUTURE

What will the future hold for me
as we go into the new century?
What will the wildlife that I know be like,
will the animals still live and roam free,
will trees still grow tall and green?
I wonder if the rivers will still be clean
and will our seas be full of fish?
How about pollution and the air we breath,
will it be dirty, will it be clean,
will people ruin the countryside
by dumping their rubbish all over?
When will they stop chopping down our forests
and polluting our world?
As more and more people are born today
can we teach them to behave in a good way,
or will they run riot and kill all good ways?

Sean Gardiner (11)
Milldown Middle School

A WORLD FOR THE FUTURE

If you don't care for the world in the future
You might be in a shock.
Because if you don't care in our nature
You won't be in shock.
If you care for our nature
You must stop . . .
If you don't stop, our world will be a disaster,
So you better stop pollution forever after.

Robert Lillington (11)
Milldown Middle School

A WORLD FOR THE FUTURE

Plant some trees.
Build some houses.
What would they prefer?
The trees make oxygen.
The houses take up space.
What would they prefer?
Trees are lovely to look at.
Houses home people.
What would they prefer?
Trees make other trees
And homes for wildlife.
What do houses make?
What would they prefer?
What would be better for the future?

Peter Bellman (11)
Milldown Middle School

BOYS

Boys are loud in a crowd.
They jump and shout and mess about.
They only think of football,
And playing computer games.

I'm glad I'm a girl and I don't have to act tough,
And get dirty and messy and rough.
They're mad, they're silly,
They're boys, they're boys.

Some can be kind when they're on their own,
But when they join their friends
Their kindness ends.

Zoe Whelan (10)
Milldown Middle School

A WORLD FOR THE FUTURE

A world in the future will be computerised,
and all the people will be hypnotised.
Shops and houses will be changed,
all the world re-arranged.

Under the sea the houses will be,
all short and round.
The birds in the trees and the bumble bees,
will make a digital sound.

Metal towers big and small,
some are thin, some are tall.
Look to the future what can you see?
Copper structures, no greenery.

No telly, no jelly and all those things,
no music and all the people that sing.
School will be different,
no maths, no games.
The world will never be the same.

Daniel Palmer (11)
Milldown Middle School

BONES

Bones are gruesome and browny.
Bones are heavy and creamy white.
Bones need a life.
Bones are dirty brown.
Bones are hard and thin.
Bones are holey and flaky.
Bones are skeletons that are empty.
Bones are what we need.

Edward Saunders (10)
Milldown Middle School

GIRLS ON BOYS

Hi, we're the girls,
They are the boys;
We think they
Make too much noise.

Shouting and yelling
And messing around,
Pushing and shoving
So they fall on the ground.

Thumping and fighting
As they roll on the grass;
Getting into trouble
When being late for class.

Laughing and sniggering
If we make a mistake.
Swinging on their chairs
At lunchtime scoffing cake.

In the afternoon
They are just the same,
Shouting and talking
As though it's a game.

We've had enough,
By the end of the day.
Girls wish boys would
Go away!

Madeleine Barrett (10)
Milldown Middle School

I'D LIKE TO BE

When I get big I'd like to be:

a honey bear that climbs up trees,
a monkey that likes to swing,
or a laughing hyena that makes a din.

A donkey that gives children rides,
a penguin that really likes to slide,
or a bottlenosed dolphin who loves to dive.

When I grow up I'd like to be mummy's baby,
    'Tee hee hee.'

Charlotte Bulpitt (10)
Milldown Middle School

THE RESCUED COLT

I am a young colt,
without a fault.
My fuel is hay,
and my name is Zay.
My hooves are hard,
I was rescued from the knacker's yard,
Because of my limping leg.
I live in a warm stable now,
with my friend the cow.
The cow is called Hail,
she chews on my tail,
what a bad habit she has!

Natalie Seaford-England (11)
Milldown Middle School

STARGATE

Original handy work.
Putting every second into it
Every day.
Night comes around and still in the garage.

Stargate is now
The latest breakthrough
And it's cool!
Ready, put on the power.
Get your stuff together
And jump through
The Stargate.
Even though we may die, let's go!

Never in my life have I been so fast
Over different dimensions.
Why on earth did I come?

Jonathan Edwards (11)
Milldown Middle School

KITTENS AND CATS

Cats, cats they're so cool
Fish, fish that's what they like
Especially not with chips.

Kittens, kittens they're so cool
But they're so small
They hide in mouse holes,
Behind the sofa, anywhere
That's what kittens are for.

Vicky Crane (10)
Milldown Middle School

NEXT WORLD DREAMS

In my dreams
I meet a big, dark, silent stallion,
He was startled by my presence,
But as I approach,
He whined a greeting,
His muscles rippled in the cold night air,
I found myself upon his back,
I was flying over the ground,
It was the most extraordinary feeling,
Drumming hoof beats in my ears,
The wind whistling through my hair,
Then we stop by the moonlit lake,
With the stars' reflection on the surface like daisies,
Then the water folk come out and sing,
A lullaby so sweet and trill,
I fall asleep,
And wake up to the warm sound of our world.

Hannah Powell-Bailey (10)
Milldown Middle School

RABBITS

Rabbits are sweet
And so are you
But I like rabbits more than you
But you're my friend
I'll be there with my rabbit
Till the end.

Hayley Moors (10)
Milldown Middle School

Colours

What is blue?
The sky is blue with the lightness of the sun.
What is white?
The swans are white gliding on water.
What is black?
Blackbirds, crows and depressing moments are black.
What is red?
Anger is red and fuming fire.
What is green?
Fields are green when they're slimy.
What is yellow?
Happiness is yellow and also some plants too.
What is pink?
Why, our faces are pink but sometimes red with embarrassment.
What is brown?
Most horses are brown.

Kirsty Upward (9)
Milldown Middle School

Aircraft Carrier

When an aircraft carrier enters a port,
It looks the opposite from rather short.
A hundred and 80 metres long and 50 metres wide.
If you are the enemy, hurry up and hide.

Jump jets and helicopters flying overhead,
Here comes a bomb
Caboom . . .
You're dead!

Jamie Adams (11)
Milldown Middle School

ATHLETICS

Running, sprinting, jumping high,
Trying to reach the sky,
Trying to break a new world record,
Trying to jump very high.

Running, hurdling,
That's what I like,
Trying to win a race,
But I was off the pace.

Throwing, jumping,
Going well,
It's the last lap,
Heard the bell.

I got to the finish,
I did not win,
But I enjoyed it,
Ding, dong, ding.

Sarah Tapper (11)
Milldown Middle School

RABBITS

Rabbits are sweet and fluffy,
But they bite sometimes.
Bunch of food chucked in the cage,
In the rabbit's tummy it goes.
Then they go to bed,
See them sleep all night.

Hollie Beaumont (11)
Milldown Middle School

MY CATS

Tom is a cat
tabby is he
he's an animal companion
for my mum and me.

Tom has a brother
he's tabby and white
his name is Reg
he sleeps with me at night.

Fluffy and warm
they love lots of fuss
it's great to have animals
living with us!

Becky Nankervis (10)
Milldown Middle School

BONES

Bones are smooth,
Bones are cool,
Bones feel spooky,
Bones break,
Bones rot,
Bones join at joints,
Bones shatter,
Bones never *disappear!*

Ben Ellis (11)
Milldown Middle School

COLOURS

Blue flowers
in the sad blue sky.

Yellow sun.
Yellow feet,
on soft yellow sand.

Red roses,
red poppies,
next to hot red wine.

Green grapes,
fallen on soft,
spiky, green grass.

Black shadows,
creeping in black alleyways,
on a black
cold night.

White snow.
Bright children throwing,
white snowballs,
on a white cold day.

Pink is light,
as light as a feather.
A pink rose leaf
falls off with a flutter

Charlotte Howell (10)
Milldown Middle School

Colour Poetry

What is pink?
Pink is love
Hugs and kisses
A bedroom
What is red?
Red is freshly picked roses
And tropical fish
What is blue?
Blue is the cold frost
The sky with white fluffy clouds
What is white?
White is the snow
The ice
What is yellow?
Yellow is the sun setting in the hills
Laa-Laa the Teletubby
What is green?
Green is for green grassy hills.

Charlotte Fowler (10)
Milldown Middle School

Owls

Owls are sweet
they think so too
they think of others
just like you.

Most are brown
some are white
it depends on
the time of night.

Hayley Froud (11)
Milldown Middle School

COLOURS

What is pink?
Pink is beautiful. It is the colour of my quick start and my skin.
It is the colour of my maths book too. It makes me very happy,
never makes me sad.

What is red?
Red is really hot. Red makes me really mad. It is the colour of
lots of roses. It makes me feel like I have got lots and lots of lipstick.

What is blue?
Blue is my pencil case. It is like the big wavy sea.
Blue is a swing swinging side to side.

White is white?
White is a sheep and cloud, paper and rubber.
White makes me feel like I'm in the clouds.

What is yellow?
Yellow is the big, big sun and yellow is a pen and pencil.
Yellow makes me feel like I'm in the sun.

What is green?
Green is the grass waving side to side and the colour of kestrels.
It makes me feel like a very tall piece of grass.

Kim Cornelius (10)
Milldown Middle School

COLOURS

Red is a fuming hot and boiling colour.
Blue is a cold and freezing colour.
But black is the most boring out of any colour in the world.
Pink is a bright colour and cheerful, and it even makes you laugh.
My feelings to all of these colours are that red is a really happy
and cheerful colour, blue is really cold and lonely feeling.
Black is a dark, gloomy dungeon with dragons and a nice pinkie
colour is bright and a really cheerful colour.

Katie Royal (10)
Milldown Middle School

COLOURS

What is pink?
Pink is the colour of a pig,
a big fat smelly pig.
What is red?
Red is the colour of a rose,
a rose in a flower bed.
What is blue?
Blue is the colour of the sky,
the sky that rivers the world.

Vicki Armstrong (10)
Milldown Middle School

NIKE!

Nike is cool,
It is the best,
Kickin' the rest,
Eating the best.

David Hamilton-Lawrence (10)
Milldown Middle School

RED

Red is danger, red is stop,
Red is the colour of a chimney pot.
Red is madness, red is stressed,
Red is a bow tie that you wear for best.
Red is Mars up so high you can't see it with your own eye.
Red is love, red is hearts,
Red is like some strawberry jam tarts.
Red is a volcano with lava storming out.
Red is a field of poppies blowing in the wind.
Red is red.

Jenny Lawson (10)
Milldown Middle School

YELLOW

Yellow on a bright summer's day, joyful in every way.
The beach is yellow and so is the sun.
A yellow banana hanging from a tree.
Daffodils sitting in the garden.
Lava erupting from a volcano.
Daisies in the spring.
Butter on a piece of bread, it makes me hungry
and happy when I've eaten it.

Joe Chandler (10)
Milldown Middle School

WEATHER

The sun is hot and yellow
Changing all the time
Summer days are really hot
Because of the hot, bright sun

The rain is cold and wet
Changing all the time
Winter days are quite wet
Because of the watery rain

The snow is cold and white
Changing all the time
Winter days can be white
Because of the frozen snow

The wind is strong and can be cold
Changing all the time
Winter days and summer days can have strong wind or cold days
Because of the wind which can be strong or calm.

Nikki Wade (10)
Milldown Middle School

WOODLAND

I like the noise of the leaves
and the green of the trees.
The movement of the animals
as they dart here and there.
We pass the River Stour,
it took an hour.
As the insects buzzing here
and there on the water.

David Judd (10)
Milldown Middle School

ON SATURDAY MORNING

Saturday morning is
All so busy
Everyone shouting
Everyone whizzy
Stomping, screaming
All around the house
Nobody is as quiet as a mouse
Running, jumping
Hopping everywhere
Never is there any time to spare
Saturday morning is
All so busy
Everyone shouting
Everyone whizzy
Stomping, screaming
All around the house
Nobody is as quiet as a mouse
Everybody
Everybody
Oh do shut up
Otherwise we
Will never get out into all
The riot
Oh please be
Quiet.

Emma Christopher (10)
Milldown Middle School

ALIEN SOCCER

One day I was playing football,
I saw something in the sky,
I was beamed up by a UFO,
As I went I shouted 'Bye!'

The captain looked at me,
He stood there green and tall,
'I never wanted you,
I meant to get the ball!'

We got near to the surface,
We landed on planet Mars,
The football is different here,
The goals have no crossbars!

I joined in a game,
And hit one on the volley,
The goalie simply stood there,
'Catch it,' shouted Wally!

As the whistle went,
And ended my game on Mars,
I realised one of my ambitions,
To play football with the stars!

Nicholas Stringer (10)
Milldown Middle School

RAINBOW COLOURS

Red is a rose,
Always staying red,
Never changing,
Roses are red.

Yellow is a sun,
Always shining yellow,
As bright as anything,
Suns are yellow.

Pink is a bow,
Bows are usually pink,
Pigs are pink,
Babies can be pink.

Green is the grass,
Leaves are green,
Cats' eyes are green,
Grass is always green.

Purple is a flower,
Purple is a purple pencil,
Purple pencils colour flowers,
Flowers are purple.

Orange is an orange,
Oranges are fruit,
Oranges taste nice,
I like to eat an orange.

Blue is the sky,
Blue is cold,
Blue is water,
The sky is blue.

Lucy Parsons (10)
Milldown Middle School

COLOUR

Red is for blood
Blue is for water
Green is for grass
White is for ghosts
Yellow is for bananas
Black is for badness
Orange is for oranges
Pink is for skin
Brown is for bark
Gold is for 1st place
Silver is for 2nd place
Bronze is for 3rd place
Indigo is for Bahamas' water.

Matthew Chapman (10)
Milldown Middle School

GOAL IN THE FINAL!

Corner ball for England,
David Beckham steps up to take it,
I'm not so sure,
Do we need Bobby Moore?
Or will David Beckham make it?
He chips it high,
Will we be off-side?
Or will it be in the net?
The opposition clear it,
The manager starts to threat,
Ian Wright chips it high,
Shearer takes a brilliant strike,
Yes, it's in the back of the net!

Clive Coats (10)
Milldown Middle School

COLOUR

Red is for roses.
Green is for leaves.
Yellow is for bananas.
White is for ghosts.
Blue is for sky.
Orange is for oranges.
Purple is for lavender.
Pink is for skin.
Gold is for gold nuggets.
Silver is for fool's gold.
Black is for night sky.
Brown is for chocolate.
Indigo is for flowers.

Christopher Kerley (10)
Milldown Middle School

EASTER

Easter is good
You get yummy eggs
Made out of chocolate
Smartie eggs are my favourite
They never end
I always send one to my friend
Maybe I will get one this year, who knows?
I hope I do
I eat my Easter egg bit by bit
Yummy, yummy for my tummy.

Amy Ellis (11)
Milldown Middle School

COLOUR POETRY

Yellow is bright and colourful like the blazing fire sun, like a juicy lemon too. Stars are yellow, so are spring daffodils too!

Blue's nice and cool like water. The sky is very pale blue with bobbing fluffy clouds. Dolphins and big whales are a navy blue just like our uniform! Blue makes people think of sadness and coldness like freezing icicles.

Red is for hearts, love and royal carpets. It's angry and hot like a burning, exciting fire, eating up anything.

Green is fresh and minty, like green fields and crunchy grass and smelly, wet seaweed too. It's fresh for spring and creepy crawlies.

Pink is for baby girls and beautiful bows in hair. Pink's not for boys said my brother over there. Pink's for nice weddings and lily flowers.

Grey is dull like a horrid, rainy day. Grey's for thunder and for sadness and smoky grey roads.

Zara Hanson (10)
Milldown Middle School

RED

Red is for lots of things like fire.
Red is for warning signs.
You can have red pens.
Red is for evil.
You can get red flowers.
You can get red hats.
Red is a nice colour.
Red is my favourite colour.

Tanya Williams (10)
Milldown Middle School

THE OLD HOUSE

It sits upon the hill,
        looking old and worn.
The curtains in the windows,
        are dusty and torn.
Nobody lives there,
        no one would dare.
I don't think I,
        would like to live there.

The garage is old,
        and totally bare.
I wonder who,
        used to live there.
The garden is always,
        covered in mist.
Who could leave,
        a garden like this?

Samantha Cooper (11)
Milldown Middle School

COLOURS OF THE WORLD

In the rose bush they are red with a yellow smell.
Floating around in the blue sky is a buzzing bumble bee.
In a country a flag waving in the sun, it's shining yellow
and the grass raised up green underneath brown muddy patching.
Why is sand so brightly yellow and shining golden?
Blue sea and a ship with an orange banner.
If you see a whale make sure it's blue.
When you paint think of some things of the colour that you are using.

Hamish Hogg (10)
Milldown Middle School

GETTING RID OF THE DOG

The whistle has just gone,
We have maths first,
But I'm not concentrating,
I cannot stop thinking about the dog,
We have to get rid of him today,
Is he gone, or is he still there?
School over, I'm glad,
I walk home very slowly,
Still thinking about the dog,
I open the door to my house,
And it's all quiet,
I sit and I cry.

Claire Fowkes (11)
Milldown Middle School

CLIO

I love my car called Clio,
When I'm in him I eat a Trio,
But I love him lots and lots.
He can be noisy, he can be nice,
He can be as quiet as little mice,
But I love him lots and lots.
He likes my mum, he likes my dad,
He won't like my sister, he's very bad,
But I love him lots and lots.

Lorelei Dunn (10)
Milldown Middle School

WEATHER

Wind blowing here and there
Leaves, flowers and petals flying everywhere.
The wind whistling through the trees
Making quite a breeze.

Snow lightly falling down
Making no noise as it touches the ground.
The snow falls as silent as silent can be
Covering the houses, the plants and the trees.

Rain, pitter pattering on the trees and grass
Splashing in the puddles before it comes to pass.
The rain falling really fast
Possibly all night it will last.

Lucy Lake (10)
Milldown Middle School

SISTERS

Younger sisters,
Painful sisters,
Trouble making sisters,
Small, sticky sisters,
Ghostly sisters,
Terrifying sisters,
Please go away!
Younger sisters,
Messy little sisters,
Stinky sisters,
Do you have a stinky little sister too?

Jade Davis (10)
Milldown Middle School

THE COLOUR BLUE

Blue is the colour of the sky up above us.
Blue is the colour of a cold drink after a hot summer's day.
Blue is the colour of candyfloss so sticky and nice.
Blue is the colour of the sea, nice and cool with lots of fish.
Blue is the colour of lovely flowers in the summer time.
Blue is the fast sports cars whizzing by.
Blue is a ribbon long and smooth.
Blue is paper to make very fast paper aeroplanes.
Blue is the delicious blackberry sweets.
Blue is trainers to play in and to have fun.
Blue is paint to paint rooms and doors.
Blue waves in the sea that fall over you when you are playing in it.
Blue can be light bubbles to make your room feel like you are under water.
Blue makes me feel sporty because it reminds me about the England flag.
Blue is the colour of tears if someone is upset.

Malcolm Kennedy (10)
Milldown Middle School

SISTERS

S isters, sometimes sweet,
I gnore them because they're annoying,
S weets, sweets that's all they want,
T errifying; sisters wrecking your stuff,
E ndangered, I don't think they'll ever be endangered,
R ude, they think it's funny when they make rude noises,
S illy sisters, but they can be cute, I suppose.

Katie Booker (11)
Milldown Middle School

SPOTS

I like spots.
Spots are black,
Spots are white,
If they're scary,
They might give you a fright.
They live on animals,
Some on their tummy,
They look so pretty,
And kind of yummy.
I like stripes,
I like spotty,
If they're funny,
They will drive you potty.
Oh no, oh no!
They might explode,
And take over,
The entire globe.
Lakes will be spotty,
And mountains too,
Towns will be covered,
And look like goo.
They grow on your face,
And on your nose,
They stand out a mile,
And they look gross.
I hate spots!

William Marsh (11)
Milldown Middle School

What Am I?

I am furry, I am sweet
I have four legs and two ears
Floppy ones I would say
And I have a big nose on the end of my head
I can smell all sorts of funny things with it
What am I?

Debi Haines (11)
Milldown Middle School

Blue

Blue is the sea. It's also snow for me.
Blue is uniform for me. Jumpers and trousers are blue.
It makes me gloomy and cold inside.
Blue, blue, blue.

Daniel Sams (10)
Milldown Middle School

Bones

Rib bones look like crowbars.
The spine is like a snake.
Some bones stick out.
They are light as feathers.
Some the colour of milk.
Most are tough as boots.

James Tapper (11)
Milldown Middle School

GREEN AND BLUE

Green is salty seaweed swaying in the sea
Blue are the waves marching in and out
Green is a slimy frog sitting on an apple
Blue is the sky with a red hot sun
Green is a hot summer's day
Blue is a cold icy day
Green peas in a green bowl
Blue blueberries or bluebells in a field
Green parrots in a tropical jungle
Blue blue tits in a dark forest saying 'Tu-whit, tu-whoo'
Green, green, green and blue, they are neat colours
don't you agree?

Hephzibah Hickish (10)
Milldown Middle School

COLOURS

What is pink? Pink is a kiss and it makes me feel very warm.
What is red? Red is boiling hot lava, it makes me feel all warm.
What is blue? Blue is the sea sparkling at me and it makes me feel all cold.
What is white? White is a dull colour like grey.
What is yellow? Yellow is a joyful colour, it reminds me of banana milkshake.
What is green? Green is spring grass and it is a warm colour too.

Sam Galvin (10)
Milldown Middle School

A Dog's Life In Colours

What is pink?
Pink is puppies out in the world for the first time.
What is red?
Red is fire warming the young dog after its walk in the rain.
What is yellow?
Yellow is a golden retriever turning gold after its puppy years.
What is blue?
Blue is the sky on an adult dog's ideal walk, the sun beating down on its back.
What is green?
Green is a dog wishing it wasn't ill on the way to the vets.
What is white?
White is an old dog turning to death.

Jo Brown (10)
Milldown Middle School

The Colour Red

Red is for anger and also for might.
Red is for love and also for a very bright rose.
Red is for sore and also for blood.
Red is for flames and also for a dangerous fire.
Red is the heart that pumps the blood around my body.
Red is the sun that floats in the sky.
Red is a tomato and for a very juicy strawberry.
The colour red makes me feel that I am in trouble.
Red is for death and also for a devil.

Martin Cox (10)
Milldown Middle School

THE COLOUR PINK

Pink is pink, not white or blue.
A bright pink sunset fades with pink clouds.
Pink baby's bottom, *phew!*
Pink is love on wedding days.
Pink puppies, pink squealing pigs.
Strawberry milkshake, candyfloss too,
Yum, yum, yum.

Pink fluffy slippers.
I go to sleep and dream my dreams.
When I wake up pink sky is here again.
Pink is love.
It's cheerful, it's jolly.
It's pink.

Jennifer Hill (10)
Milldown Middle School

BONES

As small as a fish
As big as a shark
Dusty and grey
And far too dark

Slippery and old
Dusty and white
Spiky and brown

As strong as a wall
As weak as a pin.

Samantha Herbert (11)
Milldown Middle School

THE COLOUR YELLOW

Yellow is the colour of the great big sun that twinkles above us,
Yellow is the colour of the sand on the great big beach.
Yellow is the colour of pancakes that we eat on Pancake day,
Yellow is the colour of the big smily face that comes out when Lucy gets a doll,
Yellow is the colour of happiness when someone makes your day,
Yellow is the colour of a great big glass of lemonade,
Yellow is the colour of someone with a banana,
Yellow is the colour of frightening monster horns,
Yellow is the colour of Laa-Laa from the Teletubbies.
Yellow is the colour of a hot summer's day,
Yellow is the colour of the sun setting in the sky
And now my poem has come to an end.

Lisa Scott (10)
Milldown Middle School

FIREWORKS

Missile attack, bang, pop, crack.
Look at the rocket, bing, bang, bong.
Look at the boy, using sparklers wrong.
Look at the deadly crackerjack.
Look at the rocket, bang, pop, whack.
Deadly bright rocket that's blue.
Hey look, there's another two!
Red! Green! and blues
They go in 102's.
Fireworks, fireworks, fireworks, fireworks,
They go up with a bang!
Fireworks go up and explode.
Now it's time to reload.

Mark Murnane (11)
Milldown Middle School

FIREWORKS

Loud rockets bang,
Sparkling Catherine wheels whooshing.
Dangerous missile attack, pop,
Crackling red Roman candles.

Green bangers whooshing,
Deadly screeching firecrackers.
Blue crackerjacks wheeze,
Sparkling sparklers, sssss . . . gone.

Whizzing, popping . . . rockets.
Green, blue and red rockets.
Red, raging rockets,
Deadly firecrackers, kaboom.

Rachel Wells (10)
Milldown Middle School

BONES

Bones, some look like back scratchers
Bones, they're gruesome
Bones are brain boggling
Bones, they're delicate
Bones, they need a life
Bones, they're flaky
Bones, they're holey
Bones, they're dirty grey
After all they're dead.

Chris Way (11)
Milldown Middle School

ALPHABET POEM

Poems are adventures
Poems are beautiful
Poems are cool
Poems are dippy
Poems are exciting
Poems are funny
Poems are great
Poems are happy
Poems are incredible
Poems are jazzy
Poems are for kids
Poems are loveable
Poems are magical
Poems are naughty
Poems are old
Poems are peaceful
Poems are quiet
Poems are red
Poems are for safety
Poems are tidy
Poems are understanding
Poems are about a variety of subjects
Poems aren't washable
Poems are extraordinary
Poems are young
Poems are zany.

Laura Gatehouse (10)
Milldown Middle School

BLACK LABRADOR

B lack
L azy
A rmoured
C lever
K icking

L ovely
A mazing
B est at biting
R unning about with my socks
A ccurate at football
D usky
O rdinary
R un away!

Ashley Lock (11)
Milldown Middle School

BONE

Old.
Pale white and grey,
A good structure.
It looks like an alien.
It looks smooth,
Lots of nooks and crannies.
The bones fit together like a puzzle.

Yan Lyngbo Clerc (12)
Milldown Middle School

FIREWORKS

Fireworks, fireworks are deadly dangerous.
Fireworks, fireworks go bang and crack.
Fireworks, fireworks red, blue green.
    You think that's it but then
        Bang
            Bang
                Screech!

Nathan Nicholls (10)
Milldown Middle School

JELLY

Jelly is wobbly
Jelly is wibbly
It slides all round the plate

Jelly is delicious
You can get it in all flavours
Apart from brussel sprouts.

Richard Ebborn (11)
Milldown Middle School

FIREWORKS

Sparkling Catherine wheels pop,
Loud rockets kaboom!
Blue bangers bang,
Popping red Roman candles.

Sparkling sparklers spinning splendidly,
Cream crackerjacks crackling,
Amazing bangers banging blue,
Reaching rockets roaming red.

Whizz, pop . . . Catherine wheels,
Whistle, white, whizzing rockets,
Fantastic firecrackers, fighting fast.

Deadly, dangerous, darting, dazzling Catherine wheels,
Banging, booming, bashing bangers,
Crackling, creeping, crawling . . .
                      Crackerjacks!

Samantha Francis (10)
Milldown Middle School

BONES

Bones are smooth,
Bones are light,
Bones are dead,
Bones look like backscratchers,
Bones are brain-boggling,
Bones are interesting,
Bones are thin,
Everywhere you look bones are there.

Darren Rice (10)
Milldown Middle School

SENSE OF SMELL

I love to smell my mum's perfume.
I love to smell when my mum's hoovered.
I love to smell when my mum's polished.
I love to smell the fresh grass in the morning.
I love to smell my Pantene hair conditioner.
I love to smell a fresh smell in the morning.
I love to smell juicy oranges.

Vicky Frampton (10)
Milldown Middle School

FIREWORKS

F irecrackers go bang, bang, bang.
I mpossible to get your hands on.
R ed Catherine wheels *wheee*.
E veryone cheers and claps.
W *heee* go missile attacks.
O h how cool.
R ockets go bomb, bomb, *bomb*.
K aboom say missile attacks.
S parkling sparklers sizzle, sizzle.

Daniel Harris (10)
Milldown Middle School

A SENSE OF SIGHT

I love to see the movement of the deep blue sea,
And the little fish all swimming away,
I love to see the wrinkles when you throw a stone in the water,
And I love to see the dolphins speaking to me.
I love to see the animals in their natural habitat,
Playing and dancing as the day goes by.
I love to see their new babies coming into the world.

Gemma Hunt (10)
Milldown Middle School

FIREWORKS

F un to watch
I nteresting
R oman candle
E xtraordinary
W heels
O onomatopoeia
R ockets go up, up, up, *bang!*
K aboom
S parkling stars go down to the ground.

Lemara Bugg (10)
Milldown Middle School

TEACHERS!

T eaching
E ducation
A dorable
C hildren
H istory
E ssays
R eading
S tories!

Siân Belt (10)
Milldown Middle School

PINK AND PINK

Poppies are pink.
Ice-cream is pink and yummy.
Noses are pink on our faces.
Kites are pink in the sky.

Nesta Grant (10)
Milldown Middle School

TABLES

Wooden, firm,
Round, rectangular,
Lean on it,
Write on it,
Only one problem,
    No legs!

Steven Tankard (11)
Milldown Middle School

LONDON POEM!

London lights shine at night
Orange cranes in the sky
Very bright, very high.

Canary Wharf pointed and sharp
Reaching into the sky
Very bright, very high.

Here and there and everywhere
Traffic and voices fill the air
Noisy planes in the sky
Very bright, very high.

Big Ben strikes ten
    Boom!

Amy Furness (10)
St Mary's CE VA School, Beaminster

THE CITY

L ights at night, so bright
O ver Tower Bridge into the city
N ew buildings, old buildings
D ing dong goes Big Ben
O n to the city
N ight-time never ends!

Karen Gibbs (9)
St Mary's CE VA School, Beaminster

THE MIDNIGHT HOUR

Towering London in the
Midnight hour.
Some people starving,
Some people rough,
Some in tunnels where the
Darkness bites.
People with briefcases
That snap shut tight,
Flowing crystal fountains
What a beautiful sight.
Standing tall with lights
All around Canary Wharf
In glass it towers.

Sam Ellis (10)
St Mary's CE VA School, Beaminster

EXCITING LONDON

Roaring trains through the station,
Rushing river, twisting Thames,
Clamping feet of horse parade,
Scary dark, underground.

Great gallery, paintings galore,
Fountains splashing, splash splash splash,
Hooting horns of booming traffic,
London is the best!

James Ashdown (10)
St Mary's CE VA School, Beaminster

MY FAMILY

In my family we number six,
And we love each other dearly.
Sometimes we fight but soon make up,
Because we know what's right really.

First there's mum, then there's dad,
Caroline and Paul are their names.
They're loving and caring and always there,
And always find time to join in our games.

My eldest sister is called Victoria,
Sometimes we're friends, sometimes we fight.
She takes my pens but gives me her clothes,
And goes to bed later than me at night.

Next comes me, and my name's Gemma,
I like to stay home and help in the house.
Cooking and gardening and helping my mum,
And when she is resting I'm as quiet as a mouse.

The third girl is Alex, who's only six,
She's pretty with blonde hair and brown eyes.
She torments her big sisters by day and by night,
Then when they're cross, she cries.

Last but not least, comes our brother Nick,
The youngest of us all.
A baby full of mischief and tears,
Everyone says he's going to be tall.

So this is my family, all loving and content,
Safe and secure together.
If only every child were as lucky as me,
Surrounded by love forever.

Gemma Beer (10)
St Osmond's CE School, Dorchester

THE QUEEN OF THE NIGHT

Midnight:
　　　Sparkling stars twinkle in the deep black sky,
My eye catches the moon's unworldly glimmer
As she lights up the sky with a strike of glistening silver
Which bathes the world in an unearthly glow.
The man in the moon catches my eye,
But such beauty must be feminine.
The silver path from heaven to earth becomes a
Highway for the fairy folk, as with dainty feet
They tiptoe between sleeping man and the heavens.
Our ghostly world is bathed in moonlight,
The Silver Queen draining the colour of life
Leaving us with greys, blacks, golds and silvers.
The Queen of the Night is touching the world with her silver fingertips
Whilst the stars stand around her like her handmaidens.
They follow her willingly into exile when the day comes.
They guard her when she is pale and weak
And when she loses her full shape and almost disappears
Into the face of her enemy, the sun.
In return, she thanks them by giving them her light
So they sparkle even brighter in the night sky.
She controls the seas and earthly waters,
Pulling the tides this way and that
So sailors can guide their ships by the stars, and reach port safely.
The sun may rule the day but surely,
The moon is Queen of the Night.

Victoria Beer (11)
St Osmond's CE School, Dorchester

MY LITTLE FRIEND

I have a hairy 8-legged friend,
Who's really rather nice,
He spends all day in the garden
Running away from mice.

His home is in the holly bush
Amongst the prickles as you will see,
He spins a web to catch the flies
Ready for his tea.

They're big, they're little,
They're skinny or fat,
Or sometimes really hairy.
They run across the room so fast,
They look so very scary.

They hide in corners of the room,
You don't know where they've been,
Then you notice a silver thread
And a spider you have seen.

They all have little parachutes
That help them to the ground,
It could be one or hundreds,
For they never make a sound.

So when you see a spider,
Don't look at it with hate,
For it could be very friendly
And may become your mate!

Daniel Ingram-Johnson (11)
St Thomas Garnet School, Boscombe

LEAVES

Leaves are colourful
Leaves fall everywhere
On the floor
On the grass
Leaves are very nice
Red, brown and yellow
Leaves are beautiful
Leaves can be big
Leaves can be small
The trees look beautiful
With leaves on them
Leaves are lovely
Floating from the sky.

Katherine Saunders (10)
St Thomas Garnet School, Boscombe

FIRE

Blazing red flames
Burning hot,
It seems to me
Like it's making a plot.

A plot to make us
Cosy and warm,
It's burning hot
And seems to spread and swarm.

Keeping our fingers and toes
Out of the cold,
The colour is red,
Orange and gold.

Jessica Reeves (10)
St Thomas Garnet School, Boscombe

HAPPINESS IS

When I play.
Playing piano.
No homework.
Going on holiday.
Having lots of friends.
Riding my bike.
Taking my dogs for a walk.
Going skiing.
Having pocket money.
Going swimming.

Amy Stokes (10)
St Thomas Garnet School, Boscombe

THE INVASION

I've got a really cool game,
In which aliens from outer space came.
You have to blast them out of the sky,
I wonder why?
I think they want to wipe out the human race.

They'll have to try really hard,
Shall I send them a funeral card?
I'll shoot them with my super gun,
It really weighs a ton!
Hey, look they've gone,
I think we've won!

Ishaan Chauhan (10)
St Thomas Garnet School, Boscombe

HALF-TERM BREAK

Nothing to do,
Nowhere to go,
No friends,
How I feel low.

Up early - off out,
How things turn about.
In the car off we go,
There is swimming,
Splashing, screaming,
What fun!

There's running,
There's jumping,
We all roll about,
Everyone's happy without a doubt.
Days of endless excitement,
The holiday's over,
Now work must begin.

John Henwood (11)
St Thomas Garnet School, Boscombe

TOAD

As I was wandering down the road
I saw a funny sight,
A great big green and slimy toad
Was flying a yellow kite.

I passed him by with a cheery wave
He croaked a bright 'Hello',
But then the wind began to blow
And so the toad took flight.

Nicholas Baker (10)
St Thomas Garnet School, Boscombe

LOST AND FOUND

One day I was playing with my shadow,
When Mother said to come inside,
'It's time for dinner.' she said.
But when I came outside again my shadow was gone!

I looked under the swing,
Behind the shed,
And even in the bushes
But my shadow was gone!

Mother said to come inside
'It's getting dark,' she said.
So, I went to bed . . . without my shadow.

This morning,
I got out of bed without my shadow,
I got dressed without my shadow,
Ate breakfast without my shadow,
And went to school without my shadow.

But when I came home to look for my shadow,
I found it
Right behind me!

Alexandra Hixson (10)
St Thomas Garnet School, Boscombe

WHY I LOVE YOU

Why I love you,
I do not know,
but maybe it's your personality,
that makes me go!

Why I love you,
Oh I know now!
It's your good looks
that make me go *wow!*

Why I love you,
I know I do!
It is simply because . . .
I just do!

Lucy Barfoot (10)
St Thomas Garnet School, Boscombe

WEATHER

The snow is falling to the ground,
The wind is blowing round and round,
The people are shivering in the cold,
The storm is shouting through the clouds.
Wrap up warm and stay indoors,
Until the storm breaks away.
The sun is shining,
People are smiling,
What a lovely day.

Charlene Mackin (10)
St Thomas Garnet School, Boscombe

SEASIDE

The sun shines brightly over the sea,
And the seagulls seem to be watching me.
The sea is calm,
The sand is soft,
I'll dig a hole with my bucket and spade,
Then I'll go into our sea-blue painted beach hut,
That will give more shade.

The sun goes down,
The sea becomes calm,
And now there's no use for my sun balm.
It's starting to rain,
And it's getting dark,
I'd better go home and thank goodness I haven't seen a shark.

Sarah Linda (10)
St Thomas Garnet School, Boscombe

COMMUNICATION?

Computer technology, that's the name of the game.
The world's never going to be the same.
With E-mail, faxes and the Internet,
Are we going to deserve what we get?
Personal relationships, contact eye to eye,
Replaced by wire connections and the press of keys.
Oh dear! I'd rather stay computer-free *please!*

Thomas Leonard (10)
St Thomas Garnet School, Boscombe

NOISES

Train tracks clatter,
Children chatter,
Thunder crash
after a lightning flash,
Noises!

Rain that lashes,
Water splashes,
Wind that rattles,
A seagull cackles,
Noises!

Music blaring,
Paper tearing,
Babies crying,
Adults sighing,
Noises!

Doors that slam,
A whistling tram,
All these noises,
Then . . . silence!

Phillip Sawyer (10)
St Thomas Garnet School, Boscombe

SHARK ATTACKS

With surfboards and lilos they make their own way
On to the beach to spend a fun day.
'Last one in is a sissy.' You hear a boy cry.
'The water is lovely, come in have a try!'

With lilos and rings and surfboards too,
You can hear them all yell 'We're coming on through.'
They laugh and they scream with obvious delight,
Riding the waves with all of their might.

The waves crash around them and on to the shore.
Retrieving their surfboards they call out for 'More!'
But danger is lurking up on the horizon.
The boys have no thoughts for the danger they're in.

The menacing shadow looms very near.
The boys turn quickly and at once there is fear.
'Swim for your lives, there's danger within!'
As one of them spots the trail of the fin.

With legs and arms thrashing
The waves send them crashing
Up onto the shore.
And all of a sudden, the fun is no more!

The boys lie exhausted and totally shaken.
The surfboards and lilos all twisted and broken.
They pick themselves up off the soggy wet sand,
And realise how lucky, they were not to have drowned.

The fin of the shark disappears out of sight.
Shock sets in as they tremble with fright.
The day at the beach is over and done.
It's the shark who has really had all of the fun!

Darren Head (10)
St Thomas Garnet School, Boscombe

THE TRAVELLER ON THE COAST

I see the fisherman all talk
I hear the oystercatchers squawk,
I smell the stink of fresh caught fish,
I taste the food upon my dish,
I feel the warmth of a blazing fire,

He said 'I see the fishermen talk,
    I hear the oystercatchers squawk,
    I smell the stink of fresh caught fish,
    I taste the ones upon my dish,
    I feel the warmth of a small campfire,
    But my aches and pains are dire,
    My toes are numb, my feet are sore,
    I don't think I can walk much more.'
    But for the worst I feared,
    He walked away and disappeared.

Georgina Timmis (10)
Sherborne Preparatory School

DEATH

She fears not love, but death's request,
The icy hands upon her breast.
But do not fear spring is nigh,
And winter is where death thou lie.

She did meet death on Christmas Day,
His icy hands carried her away.
Her body has rotted into dust,
But her soul is in God's trust.

Joshua Edelman (9)
Sherborne Preparatory School

WINTER

Winter is the time of year with colours,
Every little bird flutters, collecting berries for
eating in hibernation.
Everyone will be out fishing
maybe some are Christmas wishing
The time has come
the chimney is full
What is there?
It might even be a bear
The dog is barking up at that bear
Goodness, gracious Father Christmas is in there
so it isn't a bear.
The next morning I open my stocking,
next thing I see is a big brown bear.

Christopher Ockleton   (10)
Sherborne Preparatory School

FOG

A grey fairyland hovers above the ground,
It looms around valleys,
But never moves very far,
The sun heats the ground, the fog starts to lift,
The secret fairyland goes in a drift,
The fog.

The land is not real. It's there for a bit,
We pass it every morning,
We see all the shades from white to grey,
The fog.

Ben Bradish-Ellames (10)
Sherborne Preparatory School

DIVING

Diving is a fun sport,
Wet suits always taut,
For lurking in the water's hatch,
Unexpected fish that catch.

While you are swimming up above,
Certain fish may fall in love.
The tender juicy flesh on you,
May lie in wait for someone new.

Big fish are vicious,
For that you must beware,
But smaller have ambitions,
That you may even wear!

When you put on your frog-like flippers,
Unknown fish may take a fancy to the kickers,
Why you? Beware, you beware!
They could even take your underwear!

When you dive far out to sea,
Who knows what fish there might be,
I'll tell you now for ever more,
Do not swim too far from shore,
For some fish have the strangest taste,
And won't let anything go to waste.

Jack Adams (10)
Sherborne Preparatory School

THE TIGER

I look through the trees,
And what do I see,
A beautiful tiger waiting for me,
I am alone,
So I want to run home,
But I stay well away,
From the beautiful creature I fear.

His eyes are green,
And mine are blue,
We stare at each other for a minute or two,
He takes a pace forward,
I take a pace back,
I hear a gun go crackety-crack.

The tiger lies dead,
My eyes fill with tears,
The tiger is gone,
Who really cares?

George Smibert (10)
Sherborne Preparatory School